Compliments

of

First Christian Church

Decatur, Alabama

D0064326

Best Friends Last A Lifetime

Best Friends
Last A
Lifetime

S. M. Henriques
(known to his friends as "Rocky")

WALNUT GROVE PRESS, Nashville, TN 37211
1-800-256-8584

ISBN 1-58334-033-5

The quoted ideas expressed in this book (but not Scripture verses) are not, in all cases, exact quotations, as some have been edited for clarity and brevity. In all cases, the author has attempted to maintain the speaker's original intent. In some cases, quoted material for this book was obtained from secondary sources, primarily print media. While every effort was made to ensure the accuracy of these sources, the accuracy cannot be guaranteed. For additions, deletions, corrections or clarifications in future editions of this text, please write WALNUT GROVE PRESS.

Printed in the United States of America.

Layout by Swan Lake Communications, Jackson, Mississippi
Cover Design by Bart Dawson

Scripture passages marked (NIV) are taken from the HOLY BIBLE, NEW INTERNATIONAL VERSION ©. NIV ©. Copyright © 1973, 1978, 1984, by International Bible Society. Used by permission of Zondervan Publishing House. All rights reserved.

Scripture verses marked (NLT) are taken from the Holy Bible, New Living Translation, copyright © 1996. Used by permission of Tyndale House Publishers, Inc., Wheaton, Illinois 60189. All rights reserved.

Scripture verses marked (TLB) are taken from the The Living Bible, copyright 1971. Used by permission of Tyndale House Publishers, Inc., Wheaton, Illinois 60189. All rights reserved.

For my true friends,
who proved their friendship
when it really cost them something to do so;
who have stood by, offering help,
strength and encouragement whenever possible;
who have refused to believe the worst;
who would not look the other way;
who know my faults and weaknesses
and love me anyway —

Your number is too few,
but many more than I deserve.
Thank you.

Best friend,
my well-spring in the wilderness!

GEORGE ELIOT

Table of Contents

*My father always used to say
that when you die, if you've got
five real friends, then you've
had a great life.*

LEE IACOCCA

Introduction

This is a book about friendship. In here you'll find the thoughts and words of men and women who discovered the real value of having, and being, a friend. As you read, you'll be challenged to examine your own understanding of friendship, as well as to celebrate this most wonderful of gifts.

There are several reasons for reading a book like this. Perhaps you'll find some inspiration here which will help you better appreciate the friends who are currently in your life. Maybe you'll be motivated to more clearly express your love and friendship for others. Or perhaps you'll be encouraged to go out and make a new friend.

Regardless, you'll discover some great ideas about the relationships which keep most of us going. Ponder them. Meditate over them. Take them into your heart and soul. And let them encourage and motivate you.

We'll start by rediscovering how to spot a friend. We'll briefly explore the value of friendship, before looking at some of the finer points of being and keeping a friend. True friends deserve a chapter all of their own! Nothing is quite like a friendship which has lasted through the years, so we'll take time to remember those.

Explore the miscellaneous words of wisdom on friendship which have been collected here — and go out and make some friends!

ભ

A friend is someone
who laughs at your jokes
when they're not very funny
and sympathizes with your problems
when they're not very serious.

UNKNOWN

ONE

How To Spot A Friend

What is a friend? There are a lot of opinions. Most of us have what we consider to be pretty good ideas, yet when pressed to give a definition, we find it difficult to express in words. A few characteristics of friendship we seem to know by instinct; others, only after much experience.

A. P. Stanley once set out to define friendship, but soon found the task too difficult. He found it best to describe the concept using word pictures. I tend to agree. Here are some of them:

> *Like music heard on the waters,*
> *Like pines when the wind passeth by,*
> *Like pearls in the depths of the ocean,*
> *Like stars that enamel the sky,*
> *Like June and the odor of roses,*
> *Like dew and the freshness of morn,*
> *Like sunshine that kisseth the clover,*
> *Like tassels of silk on the corn . . .*

When you read those, the name and face of a dear friend probably came to mind. Read on to discover how others have tried to define that very special gift to humankind called "Friendship."

ॐ

A friend is not only a rock of shelter to us in time of danger, but is also as rivers of water in a thirsty land, when our hearts cry out for life and love.

J. R. MILLER

A friend is a person with whom I may
be sincere. Before him I may think aloud.
Ralph Waldo Emerson

You can always tell a real friend;
when you've made a fool of yourself, he
doesn't feel you've done a permanent job.
Laurence J. Peter

The best times in life are
made a thousand times better
when shared with a dear friend.
Luci Swindoll

A friend is someone you can do
nothing with, and enjoy it.
Unknown

Friendship is the comfort of knowing there is
always a shoulder to lean on, a hand to reach
out for, and a heart to welcome me home.
Unknown

CR

Friends
are angels
who lift us to our feet
when our wings have
trouble remembering
how to fly.

UNKNOWN

A friend is someone who knows
the song in your heart, and can sing it
back to you when you have
forgotten the words.

Donna Roberts

A friend is one in whom we can confide.
The secret chambers of our soul open
to his touch on the latch.

J. E. Dinger

Nothing but heaven itself is better
than a friend who is really a friend.

Plautus

My friend is he who will tell me
my faults in private.

Solomon Ibn Gabirol

It is one mark of a friend that
he makes you wish to be at
your best while you are with him.

Henry Van Dyke

ભ

*Friendship
is a strong and habitual
inclination in two persons to
promote the good and happiness
of one another.*

EUSTACE BUDGELL

What is a friend? I will tell you. It is a person
with whom you dare to be yourself.

Frank Crane

Friendship: it involves many things, but,
above all, the power of going out of one's self
and seeing and appreciating whatever is noble
and loving in another.

Thomas Hughes

Friendship is the inexpressible comfort of
feeling safe with a person, having neither to
weigh thoughts nor measure words.

George Eliot

Genuine friends can enter
into our celebration with as much
or more enthusiasm as they would
have if the fortuitous serendipity
had happened to them.

Lloyd John Ogilvie

ℛ

*We cannot tell the precise moment
when friendship is formed.
As in filling a vessel drop by drop,
there is at last a drop which makes
it run over; so in a series of
kindnesses there is at last one which
makes the heart run over.*

SAMUEL JOHNSON

TWO

The Value of Friendship

Emily Dickinson once asked writer Charles Kingsley to explain the secret of his life. His answer was profound: "I had a friend."

How valuable our friendships are to us! We may not recognize their ultimate importance; we may take them for granted, not fully appreciating how much we depend on the people we count in our circle of true friends. Their value remains, nevertheless.

C. S. Lewis understood how important friendships are to us. He first wrote "Friendship is unnecessary, like philosophy, like art. . . ." But he went on to write, " It has no survival value; rather it is one of those things that give value to survival."

We might tend to disagree that friendship is not necessary, but Lewis was absolutely correct when he said that friendship is what gives value to our lives.

But I suppose my favorite description of the value of friendship comes from an author whose name is unknown to me:

> *A friend is there when everyone else isn't,*
> *Believing when everyone else hasn't,*
> *Understanding when everyone else doesn't,*
> *Loving when everyone else wasn't.*

Have you ever *known* anyone like that?
Have you ever *been* like that for anyone?

ℭℜ

*Of all happinesses,
the most charming is that of
a firm and gentle friendship.
It sweetens all our cares,
dispels our sorrows, and
counsels us in all extremities.*

S<small>ENECA</small>

Because of a friend,
life is a little stronger, fuller,
more gracious thing for the friend's
existence, whether he be near or far.
If the friend is close at hand, that is best;
but if he is far away he still is there
to think of, to wonder about, to hear from,
to write to, to share life and experience with,
to serve, to honor, to admire, to love.
Arthur Christopher Benson

Life is fortified by many friendships.
To love, and to be loved, is the
greatest happiness of existence.
Sydney Smith

Many people go far in life because
someone else thought they could.
John Maxwell

Friendship is one of the sweetest joys of life.
Charles Haddon Spurgeon

ᴄℛ

Friendship
cheers like a sunbeam;
charms like a good story;
inspires like a brave leader;
binds like a golden chain;
guides like a heavenly vision.

NEWELL DWIGHT HILLIS

All that is worth cherishing
begins in the heart, not the head.
Suzanne Chapin

A friend understands what you are
trying to say . . . even when your
thoughts aren't fitting into words.
Ann D. Parrish

A blessed thing is for any man or woman
to have a friend; one human soul whom
we can trust utterly; who knows the best
and the worst of us, and who loves us
in spite of all our faults; who will speak
the honest truth to us, while the world
flatters us to our face, and laughs at us
behind our back; who will give us counsel
and reproof in the day of prosperity and
self-conceit; but who, again, will comfort
and encourage us in the day of difficulty
and sorrow, when the world leaves us
alone to fight our own battle as we can.
Charles Kingsley

ᴄᴙ

*A friend is dearer than
the light of heaven; for it
would be better for us that
the sun were extinguished,
than that we should be
without friends.*

Sᴛ. Jᴏʜɴ Cʜʀʏsᴏsᴛᴏᴍ

Many kinds of fruit grow upon
the tree of life, but none so sweet
as friendship.

Lucy Larcom

What wealth it is to have such friends
that we cannot think of them
without elevation.

Henry David Thoreau

My friends are an oasis to me,
encouraging me to go on.
They are essential to my well-being.

Dee Brestin

What sweetness is left in life if you
take away friendship? It is like robbing
the world of the sun.

Cicero

CR

*Fame is the scentless
sunflower, with gaudy
crown of gold;
But friendship is
the breathing rose,
with sweets in every fold.*

OLIVER WENDELL HOLMES

I no doubt deserved my enemies,
but I don't believe I deserved my friends.
Walt Whitman

Friendships, family ties, the companionship
of little children . . . the intricate design
and haunting fragrance of a flower . . . the
fluted note of bird song, the glowing glory
of a sunset: the world is aflame with
things of eternal moment.
E. Margaret Clarkson

With one friend I would count
myself rich; to possess more than one,
I were rich beyond comparison.
Cyrus B. Nubbaum

The wealthiest of men is
poor and miserable if he has no friend to
whom he can disclose the secrets of his heart.
James Gibbons

ℭℜ

When friendships are real,
they are not glass threads
or frostwork, but the
solidest things we know.

RALPH WALDO EMERSON

A poor man may be said to be rich in the
midst of his poverty, so long as he enjoys
the interior sunshine of a devoted friend.
James Gibbons

I keep my friends as misers do
their treasure, because, of all the
things granted us by wisdom,
none is greater or better than friendship.
Pietro Aretino

I thank God far more for friends
than for my daily bread —
for friendship is the bread of the heart.
Mary Mitford

Of all the things which wisdom
provides to make life entirely happy,
the greatest is the possession of friendship.
Epicurus

℞

The glory of friendship
is not the outstretched hand,
nor the kindly smile
nor the joy of companionship;
it is the spirited inspiration
that comes to one when
he discovers that someone else believes
in him and is willing to trust him.

RALPH WALDO EMERSON

Friendship is the hardest thing in the world
to explain. It's not something you learn
in school. But if you haven't learned
the meaning of friendship,
you really haven't learned anything.

Muhammad Ali

No one can develop freely in this world
and find a full life without feeling
understood by at least one person.

Paul Tournier

There can be no happiness equal to
the joy of finding a heart that understands.

Victor Robinsoll

Friendship is the source of
the greatest pleasures, and
without friends even the most
agreeable pursuits become tedious.

St. Thomas Aquinas

ℭℛ

Land and sea though we tireless rove,
And follow each trail to the end,
Whatever the wealth of our treasure-trove,
The best we shall find is a friend.

JOHN J. MOMENT

THREE

Being A Friend

We all need friends all the time.

But sometimes what we need *more* is to be a friend for someone else. It might sound selfish, but it is true that offering love and friendship to another person does us as much good as anyone.

Admittedly, it is not always easy; no one ever guaranteed that it would be. But doing the difficult, just because of friendship, is itself a wonderful description of being a friend.

Sometimes being a friend requires staying up late at night when you would much rather be sleeping. Sometimes it means canceling plans to be available for someone going through a rough time.

Other times it calls for defending another when the rumors are rampant, choosing instead to believe only the best.

Or standing by when others suddenly find themselves too busy, choosing to be available for another.

Or giving advice.

Or lending an ear.

Or sitting in silence when the pain is too great for conversation.

Or cooking a special dinner.

Or any of a million things one might name.

$\mathcal{CR}$

*The best portion of
a good man's life
is in his little nameless,
unremembered acts of
kindness and of love.*

WILLIAM WORDSWORTH

Friends should consider themselves
as the sacred guardians of each other's
virtue; and the noblest testimony they
can give of their affection is the correction
of the faults of those they love.

Anna Letitia Barbauld

The man who treasures his friends
is usually solid gold himself.

Marjorie Holmes

The best vitamin for making friends:
B-1.

Source Unknown

Friendship is to be purchased only
by friendship. A man may have authority
over others, but he can never have
their hearts but by giving his own.

Thomas Wilson

ଔ

A word of kindness is seldom
spoken in vain, while witty sayings
are as easily lost as the pearls
slipping from a broken string.

GEORGE D. PRENTICE

Be gentle and patient with people.
Everybody's bruised.

Katie Lambert

A friend is someone who needs me,
trusts me, and is happy when my news
is good; someone who won't go away.

Angela Douglas

Kind words are the music of the world.
They have a power which seems to be
beyond natural causes, as though they
were some angel's song which had
lost its way and come to earth.

Frederick William Faber

The world is a rose:
smell it and pass it on
to your friends.

Persian Proverb

ભ

To laugh often and much,
to win the respect of intelligent people
and the affection of children,
to earn the appreciation of honest critics
and endure the betrayal of false friends,
to appreciate beauty,
to find the best in others,
to leave the world a bit better . . .
to know even one life has breathed
easier because you have lived.
This is to have succeeded!

RALPH WALDO EMERSON

The best relationships are built up,
like a fine lacquer finish, with the
accumulated layers of many acts of kindness.
Alan Loy McGinnis

I have wept in the night
For the shortness of sight
That to somebody's need made me blind;
But I never have yet
Felt a tinge of regret
For being a little too kind
Source Unknown

Even if it's a little thing,
do something for those who have
no need of help, something for which
you get no pay but the privilege of doing it.
Albert Schweitzer

ଓଓ

*We ought to do good to others
as simply and as naturally as a horse
runs, or a bee makes honey, or a vine
bears grapes season after season without
thinking of the grapes it has borne.*

MARCUS AURELIUS

Have you ever had your day suddenly
turn sunshiny because of a cheerful word?
Have you ever wondered if this could
be the same world, because someone
had been unexpectedly kind to you?
You can make today the same for somebody.
It is only a question of a little imagination,
a little time and trouble.

Maltbie D. Babcock

In friendship your heart is like a bell struck
every time your friend is in trouble.

Henry Ward Beecher

Wholehearted, ready laughter
heals, encourages, relaxes anyone
within hearing distance. The laughter
that springs from love makes wide
the space around it — gives room
for the loved one to enter in.
Real laughter welcomes.

Eugenia Price

ત્ર

*If we are to forgive freely,
we need a tolerance of others as
generous as that tolerance we display
toward our own errors. . . .
To extend such understanding toward
our intimates can do a great deal
to build strong friendships.*

ALAN LOY MCGINNIS

FOUR

Keeping A Friend

Hilaire Belloc once observed, *"When friendship disappears there is a space left open to that awful loneliness of the outside world which is like the cold space between the planets. It is an air in which men perish utterly."*

Ugh. Not a very welcome prospect, is it? Relax. It is actually possible to keep your friendships, and to make sure that they stay strong and viable.

But it takes work. Lots of it. It may require extra doses of patience, love, kindness and forgiveness — on both sides. It may require attention to the little details which make up everyday living.

If someone should present us with one of the largest diamonds in the world, we probably would not use it as a doorstop or a paper weight. That gem would be stored in a safe place, that it might be preserved and protected. It would be treasured and marveled over.

Our friends have already gifted us with something much more valuable and lasting than precious stones. Are we treating those friendships with care and respect, as if they were the most valuable things we own? Are they wondrous, each moment enjoyed and treasured for the thing of beauty it is?

After all, who wants to be left out in the cold nothingness between planets?

CR

To find a friend
one must close one eye
— to keep him, two.

NORMAN DOUGLAS

We must love our friends as
true amateurs love paintings;
they have their eyes perpetually fixed
on the fine parts, and see no others.

Madame d'Epinay

Hold a true friend
with both your hands.

Nigerian Proverb

Friendships are valuable, but to flourish
they must be based on commitment.

Sheri Curry

If we advance through life and do
not make friends, we shall soon find
ourselves alone. We must keep
our friendships in constant repair.

Samuel Johnson

೧

Do not waste time bothering
whether you "love" your neighbor;
act as if you did. As soon as we do this
we find one of the great secrets.
When you are behaving as if you
loved someone, you will presently
come to love him.

C. S. LEWIS

A friendship can weather most things
and thrive in thin soil — but it needs
a little mulch of letters and phone calls
and small silly presents every so often —
just to save it from drying out completely.

Pam Brown

In the sweetness of friendship let there
be laughter, and sharing of pleasures.

Kahlil Gibran

Live so that your friends can
defend you but never have to.

Arnold H. Glasgow

When we really love others, we accept
them as they are. We make our love
visible through little acts of kindness,
shared activities, words of praise and thanks,
and our willingness to get along with them.

Edward E. Ford

CR

*I expect to pass through
this life but once. If, therefore,
there be any kindness I can show,
or any good thing I can do to any
fellow being, let me do it now,
and not defer or neglect it, as
I shall not pass this way again.*

WILLIAM PENN

Friendships are fragile things, and
require as much handling as any
other fragile and precious thing.

Randolph S. Bourne

You may be deceived if you
trust too much, but you will live
in torment if you do not trust enough.

Dr. Frank Crane

If you can help anybody even a little, be glad;
up the steps of usefulness and kindness, God
will lead you on to happiness and friendship.

Maltbie D. Babcock

ௐ

*When friendship deserts us,
we are as helpless as a ship left by
the tide high upon the shore.
When friendship returns to us, it's as
though the tide came back, giving us
buoyancy and freedom.*

HARRY EMERSON FOSDICK

Two persons cannot long
be friends if they cannot forgive
each other's little failings.

Jean De La Bruyere

Often we can help each other the most
by leaving each other alone; at other
times we need the hand-grasp
and the word of cheer.

Elbert Hubbard

Your greatest pleasure is that
which rebounds from hearts
that you have made glad.

Henry Ward Beecher

Be slow to fall into friendship;
but when thou art in,
continue firm and constant.

Socrates

ℛ

There are those who pass like ships in the night
Who meet for a moment, then sail out of sight
With never a backwards glance of regret
Folks we know briefly then quickly forget

....

Then there are those friends who sail together
Through quiet waters and stormy weather
Helping each other through joy and through strife
And they are the kind that give meaning to life.

AUTHOR UNKNOWN

FIVE

New Friends

One of the greatest pleasures of life is making a new friend. Such an event gives us a feeling of rare accomplishment, because deep inside we know that it just doesn't happen every day. Sometimes not every year.

Friendship is such a marvel because somehow we recognize it should not be tossed around indiscriminately. We reserve the best for someone we can really trust and truly love.

It is not something we should ever rush into. Friendship is not for the squeamish or the weak at heart! Why? Because of the potential perils involved.

Emma Stacy once revealed the tremendous risk we take when making friends, when she wrote, "A new friendship is like an unripened fruit — it may become either an orange or a lemon."

That is certainly true. But there is such a wealth of joy and pleasure in one friendship which stands tall against adversity, misunderstandings, illness and time that it is well worth any risk.

How sad to think of what might have been —
So, go! Take a chance and make a friend!
Rocky Henriques

಄

*There are some men
and women in whose
company we are always
at our best. All the best stops
in our nature are drawn out,
and we hear a music in
our souls never felt before.*

HENRY DRUMMOND

How rare and wonderful
is that flash of a moment when
we realize we have discovered a friend.

William Rotsler

Since there is nothing
so well worth having
as friends, never lose a
chance to make them.

Francesco Guicciardini

Two may talk together under
the same roof for many years, yet never
really meet; and two others at first
speech are old friends.

Mary Catherwood

Friendship is born at that moment when
one person says to another, "What! You too?
I thought I was the only one!"

C. S. Lewis

೧

A loyal friend is like
a safe shelter;
find one, and you have
found a treasure.

SIRACH

It is always good to know,
if only in passing,
a charming human being;
it refreshes our lives like flowers
and woods and clear brooks.

George Eliot

It is always wise to stop wishing for
things long enough to enjoy the
fragrance of those now flowering.

Patrice Gifford

No love, no friendship can cross
the path of our destiny without leaving
some mark on it forever.

François Mauriac

Your friends will know you better in
the first minute they meet you than
your acquaintances will know you
in a thousand years.

Richard Bach

☙

For memory has painted this perfect day,
with colors that never fade.
And we find at the end of a perfect day,
the soul of a friend we've made.

CARRIE JACOBS BOND

Friendship is won, not by the giving
of things, but by the giving of the heart.

Roy Lessin

Other blessings may be taken away,
but if we have acquired a good friend
by goodness, we have a blessing which
improves in value when others fail.

William Ellery Channing

You don't just luck into things
as much as you'd like to think you do.
You build step by step, whether it's
friendships or opportunities.

Barbara Bush

A true friend is the greatest of
all blessings, and that which we take
the least care to acquire.

François De La Rochefoucauld

ℂℜ

*Yes'm, old friends is always the best,
'less you can catch a new one that's
fit to make an old one out of.*

SARAH ORNE JEWETT

Do not let your vanity and self-love make you
suppose that people become your friends at
first sight, or even upon a short acquaintance.
Real friendship is a slow grower.

Lord Chesterfield

Wishing to be friends is quick work, but
friendship is a slow-ripening fruit.

Aristotle

True friendship is a plant
of slow growth, and must undergo
and withstand the shocks of
adversity before it is
entitled to the appellation.

George Washington

There is no surprise more magical
than the surprise of being loved.

Margaret Kennedy

೧

Sometimes, when you are really in need,
you will have a few friends who will say to you,
"I'll do whatever you wish. I'm available."
No one will ever know about them, but they'll
run interference for you. They'll be down there
at the front lines, where it isn't really pleasant,
protecting you from the blast, shielding and
encouraging you just by their presence there.
It may work against them; they may get beat up
by those who have turned against you . . .
but there they stand, in your corner.
They are friends.

CHARLES SWINDOLL

SIX

True Friends

As the football coach at UCLA some time ago, Pepper Rodgers was having one particularly bad year. Many were calling for his resignation or dismissal.

He remarked later: "My dog was my only friend. I told my wife that every man needs at least two friends. She bought me another dog."

While Rodgers probably told that story for its comic value, he underscored a truth about friendship all of us would do well to think about. A real friend is true, no matter the circumstances.

Mere acquaintances may stay long enough to enjoy your company and allow you to enjoy theirs; they may have a genuine feeling of comradeship when around you; you may even share similar tastes and opinions.

A true friend, on the other hand, is one who sticks by you, even when others don't; who finds time for you even when there is no time left; who knows your faults, weaknesses, and personality quirks — and still loves you anyway.

The Old Testament book of Proverbs contains this insight into friendship:

> *There are "friends" who destroy each other,*
> *but a real friend sticks closer than a brother.*
> Proverbs 18:24 (NLT)

ᚱ

*Sometimes our light goes out
but is blown into flame by another
human being. Each of us owes
deepest thanks to those
who have rekindled this light.*

ALBERT SCHWEITZER

Truly great friends are
hard to find, difficult to leave,
and impossible to forget.

G. Randolf

Friends show their love in times of trouble.

Euripides

A true friend is someone
who thinks that you are a good egg
even though he knows that
you are slightly cracked.

Bernard Meltzer

Every true friend is a glimpse of God.

Lucy Larcom

Many might have failed
beneath the bitterness of their trial
had they not found a friend.

Charles H. Spurgeon

CR

When true friends meet
in adverse hour,
'Tis like a sunbeam
through a shower.
A watery way an
instant seen,
The darkly closing
clouds between.

SIR WALTER SCOTT

True friends are people
who care for one another more
"in spite of" than "because of."
Betty Carlson

A true friend is someone
who is there for you when
he'd rather be anywhere else.
Len Wein

The most beautiful discovery
true friends make is that they can grow
separately without growing apart.
Elisabeth Foley

A friend is one
who joyfully sings
with you when you are
on the mountaintop, and silently
walks with you through the valley.
William A. Ward

 og

The way to love someone
is to lightly run your finger
over that person's soul until
you find a crack, and then
gently pour your love
into that crack.

KEITH MILLER

True friends visit us in prosperity
only when invited, but in adversity
they come without invitation.

Theophrastus

No distance of place or lapse of time can
lessen the friendship of those who are
thoroughly persuaded of each other's worth.

Robert Southey

Lots of people want to ride with you
in the limo, but what you want is
someone who will take the bus with
you when the limo breaks down.

Oprah Winfrey

Indeed, we do not really live unless
we have friends surrounding us like a firm
wall against the winds of the world.

Charles Hanson Towne

☙

*It's like you're in a dungeon
and somebody locks the door from
the outside, and you can't get out.
You try your best
(you may even fake it),
but you're still in there.
And all of a sudden a friend
finds a way to climb in.*

CHARLES SWINDOLL

A true friend never gets in your way
unless you happen to be going down.

Arnold H. Glasgow

Prosperity is no just scale; adversity
is the only balance to weigh friends.

Plutarch

Trouble is a sieve through which we sift
our acquaintances. Those too big
to pass through are our friends.

Arlene Francis

The real test of friendship is:
Can you literally do nothing with the
other person? Can you enjoy together
those moments of life that are utterly simple?
They are the moments people look back
on at the end of life and number as
their most sacred experiences.

Eugene Kennedy

ᏅᎡ

The best advisers, helpers and friends,
are not always those who tell us
how to act in special cases, but who
give us, out of themselves, the ardent
spirit and desire to act right, and leave
us then, even through many blunders,
to find out what our own
form of right action is.

PHILLIPS BROOKS

There is no substitute for a friend —
someone to care,
to listen, to feel,
to comfort, and, yes,
occasionally to reprove.
True friends do that best.

Charles Swindoll

In prosperity our friends know us;
in adversity we know our friends.

John Churton Collins

A faithful friend is an image of God.

French Proverb

Sometimes there is someone who takes
time enough to listen . . . who cares about
us when we lose and who loves us
even when we're wrong.

Flavia Weedn

ॐ

*It is those who will stand
by us in trouble as well as in
prosperity, who will sympathize with
us in affliction and pour consolation
into our bosoms, that we should
prize above all others.*

HARRIET B. DAVIS MINOR

A friend is one who does not laugh
when you are in a ridiculous position.
Sir Arthur Helps

I value the friend who for me
finds time on his calendar,
but I cherish the friend
who for me does not
consult the calendar.
Robert Brault

Friends show their love in times of trouble.
Euripides

When a friend is in trouble,
don't annoy him by asking
if there is anything you can do.
Think up something
appropriate and do it.
Edgar Watson Howe

 CR

*A true friend
unbosoms freely,
advises justly,
assists readily,
adventures boldly,
takes all patiently,
defends courageously,
and continues a friend
unchangeably.*

WILLIAM PENN

Friendships are what our dreams
are made of. We hold onto each other
with its binding love. We stand close
to each other, hand in hand,
showing each other we understand.
Some friends may come and go,
but you are the truest friend I know.

Elsa Maxwell

The friend of my adversity I shall
always cherish most. I can better trust
those who helped to relieve the gloom
of my dark hours than those who are
so ready to enjoy with me the
sunshine of my prosperity.

Ulysses S. Grant

Real friendship is shown in times
of trouble; prosperity is full of friends.

Euripides

ભ

Then come the wild weather,
come sleet or come snow,
we will stand by each other,
however it blow.

SIMON DACH

SEVEN

Wise Words on Friendship

Æsop once told the story of two men who were traveling together, when a bear suddenly met them on their path.

One of the men scrambled up a tree, hiding himself in the branches. The other, seeing that he would be attacked, fell flat on the ground. The bear came up and pushed at him with his snout, smelling him all over. But the man held his breath, and pretended as best he could that he was dead.

It is said that a bear will not touch a dead body. It worked, at least, in Æsop's tale. When the bear had left, the other man dropped from the tree, and jokingly asked "What was it the bear whispered in your ear?"

The one who had pretended to be dead replied, "He gave me this advice: Never travel with a friend who deserts you at the approach of danger."

Wise words. Better still for us to take them to heart, and make sure that we are not the ones scrambling up the tree when our friends need us on the ground.

If one falls down, his friend can help
him up. But pity the man who falls
and has no one to help him up!
Ecclesiastes 4:10 (NIV)

CR

*Choose your friends
carefully and wisely.
Gossips usually
gravitate to gossips.
Rebels run with rebels.
You want to be wise?
Choose wise friends.*

CHARLES SWINDOLL

A man should choose a friend who
is better than himself. There are plenty
of acquaintances in the world;
but very few real friends.

Chinese Proverb

Don't make friends who are comfortable
to be with. Make friends who will
force you to lever yourself up.

Thomas J. Watson

Friends remind us we are part
of something greater than ourselves,
a larger world, and the right
friends keep us on track.

Barbara Jenkins

The friend given you, by circumstances
over which you have no control,
was God's own gift.

Frederick Robertson

CR

I shot an arrow into the air,
It fell to earth, I knew not where;
For so swiftly it flew, the sight
Could not follow it in its flight.

I breathed a song into the air,
It fell to earth, I knew not where;
For, who has sight so keen and strong
That it can follow the flight of song?

Long, long afterward, in an oak
I found the arrow, still unbroke;
And the song, from beginning to end,
I found again in the heart of a friend.

HENRY WADSWORTH LONGFELLOW

The glory of friendship is not the
outstretched hand, nor the kindly smile,
nor the joy of companionship; it's the
spiritual inspiration that comes to one
when he discovers that someone else
believes in him and is willing to
trust him with his friendship.

Ralph Waldo Emerson

To have a friend is to have one of
the sweetest gifts that life can bring;
to be a friend is to have a solemn and
tender education of soul from day to day.

Amy Robertson Brown

Knowing what to say is not always
necessary; just the presence of a caring
friend can make a world of difference.

Sheri Curry

CB

*Nature has no love for solitude,
and always leans, as it were,
on some support; and the sweetest
support is found in the most
intimate friendship.*

CICERO

Some of the most rewarding
and beautiful moments of a friendship
happen in the unforeseen open spaces
between planned activities. It is important
that you allow these spaces to exist.

Christine Leefeldt

There is nothing better than the
encouragement of a good friend.

Katherine Hathaway

We are each of us angels with only one wing,
and we can only fly embracing each other.

Luciano De Crescenzo

If someone is too tired to give you
a smile, leave one of your own, because no
one needs a smile as much as those
who have none to give.

Rabbi Samson Raphael Hirsch

CR

*The friend who can be silent
with us in a moment of despair or
confusion, who can stay with us
in an hour of grief and bereavement,
who can tolerate not knowing,
not curing, not healing, and face us
with the reality of our powerlessness:
That is the friend who cares.*

HENRI NOUWEN

Kind words bring no blisters on the
tongue that speaks them, nor on the ear
which hears them. Kind words are never
wasted. Like scattered seeds, they spring
up in unexpected places.

Charles H. Spurgeon

It is a good and safe rule to sojourn in
every place as if you meant to spend your
life there, never omitting an opportunity
of doing a kindness, or speaking
a true word, or making a friend.

John Ruskin

The deepest of friendships will often
overrule logic. The things that would
normally come between people don't
apply because we're friends. The points
of irritation are governed by the relationship.
And the steep prices sometimes demanded
are simply worth the friendship.

Stu Weber

ᖇ

Before you speak,
ask yourself if what you are
going to say is true, is kind,
is necessary, is helpful.
If the answer is no,
maybe what you are about
to say should be left unsaid.

BERNARD MELTZER

Friends are the sunshine of life.

John Hay

The best friend is the man who in
wishing me well wishes it for my sake.

Aristotle

Friendship is a strong and habitual
inclination in two persons to promote
the good and happiness of one another.

Eustace Budgell

For the friendship of two,
the patience of one is required.

Indian Proverb

The man who treasures his friends
is usually solid gold himself.

Marjorie Holmes

CR

*Most often, broken relationships
stay broken for the lack of a patience
that will let the other person act out for
a while, allow temporary insanity in the
other for a while, and then forgive.*

ALAN LOY MCGINNIS

If we would build on a sure foundation
in friendship, we must love our friends
for their sakes rather than our own.

Charlotte Brontë

The greatest gift we can give one another is
rapt attention to one another's existence.

Sue Atchley Ebaugh

Instead of a gem, or even a flower,
if we could cast the gift of a lovely
thought into the heart of a friend, that
would be giving as the angels give.

George MacDonald

A friend is one who takes you to lunch
even though you are not tax deductible.

Unknown

 CR

*Treasure each other
in the recognition that we
do not know how long
we shall have each other.*

JOSHUA LIEBMAN

Do not save your loving speeches
For your friends till they are dead;
Do not write them on their tombstones,
Speak them rather now instead.

Anna Cummins

Whatever you want to do, do it now.
There are only so many tomorrows.

Michael Landon

Do not keep the alabaster box of
your love and friendship sealed up until
your friends are dead. Fill their lives with
sweetness. Speak approving, cheering words
while their ears can hear them, and while their
hearts can be thrilled and made happier.
The kind things you mean to say when
they are gone, say before they go.

George W. Childs

ℭℛ

Friendship:
gentle as the dew from
silken skies, radiant as
some glorious diadem,
set with countless stars.

YEOMAN SHIELD

We cannot hold a torch to light another's
path without brightening our own.

Ben Sweetland

Of all the gifts that a wise providence
grants us to make life full and happy,
friendship is the most beautiful.

Epicurus

Friendship is something that raised us
almost above humanity. . . . It is the sort
of love one imagines between angels.

C. S. Lewis

I always felt that the great high privilege,
relief and comfort of friendship was
that one had to explain nothing.

Katherine Mansfield

ᚭ

*And here is how to measure it —
the greatest love is shown
when people lay down their
lives for their friends.*

JOHN 15:13 (NLT)

It brings comfort to have
companions in whatever happens.
St. John Chrysostom

How beautiful a day can be
when kindness touches it!
George Elliston

When a friend speaks to me,
whatever he says is interesting.
Jean Renoir

I don't like that man.
I'm going to have to get to know him better.
Abraham Lincoln

I didn't find my friends;
the good Lord gave them to me.
Ralph Waldo Emerson

*There is an electricity about
a friendship relationship.
We are both more relaxed and
more sensitive, more creative
and more reflective, more energetic
and more casual, more excited and
more serene. It is as though when we
come in contact with our friend we
enter into a different environment.*

ANDREW M. GREELEY

The bird a nest,
the spider a web,
man friendship.

William Blake

One enemy is too many and
a hundred friends are too few.

Icelandic Proverb

The best times in life
are made a thousand times
better when shared with a dear friend.

Luci Swindoll

A real friend invites you to come in
even when the house is messy.

Unknown

When just being together is more important
than what you do, you are with a friend.

Unknown

༼

Oh, the comfort,
the inexpressible comfort,
of feeling safe with a person;
having neither to weigh thoughts
nor measure words, but to pour
them all out just as they are.

GEORGE ELIOT

A faithful friend is a strong defense;
and he that hath found such a
one hath found a treasure.

From *The Apocrypha*

Oh, the miraculous energy that flows
between two people who care enough to take
the risks of responding with the whole heart.

Alex Noble

Friends are kind to each other's dreams.

Henry David Thoreau

May the sun always shine on
your windowpane; may a rainbow
be certain to follow each rain.
May the hand of a friend always
be near you; may God fill your heart
with gladness to cheer you.

Irish Blessing

CR

*They are closest to us
who best understand what
life means to us, who feel
for us as we feel for ourselves,
who are bound to us in triumph
and disaster, who break the
spell of our loneliness.*

HENRY ALONZO MYERS

EIGHT

Through The Years

Few experiences in life compare to spending time with friends we've known for a long time. It may be someone we see every day, or only once in a while. We may have to depend on letter writing, phone calls or in these days, e-mail, to keep those friendships strong and healthy. Yet those relationships remain somehow unaffected by time or distance.

We don't have to prove anything with friends we've known through the years. Acceptance and understanding, mixed with generous doses of patience and loyalty, are some of the essentials for lengthy friendships.

With such friends we have history. Time has allowed us to get comfortable with one another, yet because we treasure that relationship, we never take it for granted.

Lifetime friends know how to empathize. They may not have instant solutions to offer, but it really doesn't matter, because they are there for us.

Time erodes many other relationships, but that of a true friend remains strong and tested. Time and life itself throw things at us we could not handle alone, yet somehow we make it through with the help of our friends.

Best friends really *do* last a lifetime.

ᑒ

It is great to have friends
when one is young, but indeed it is
still more so when you are getting old.
When we are young, friends are,
like everything else, a matter of course.
In the old days we know what
it means to have them.

EDWARD GRIEG

To lose an old friend is as the loss of
a bead from life's rosary; or to drop
a jewel into the depths of a turbulent sea.
Douglas Meador

Forsake not an old friend, for the
new is not comparable unto him.
From The Apocrypha

No road is long with good company.
Turkish Proverb

The holy passion of Friendship is of
so sweet and steady and loyal and enduring
a nature that it will last through a whole
lifetime, if not asked to lend money.
Mark Twain

ℭℜ

*Make the attempt if you want to, but
you will find that trying to go through life
without friendship is like milking a bear
to get cream for your morning coffee. It is
a whole lot of trouble, and then not
worth much after you get it.*

ZORA NEALE HURSTON

To be capable of steady friendship or lasting
love are the two greatest proofs, not only of
goodness of heart, but of strength of mind.
William Hazlitt

Human love and the delights of friendship,
out of which are built the memories
that endure, are also to be treasured up
as hints of what shall be hereafter.
Bede Jarrett

A life without love is like
a year without summer.
Swedish Proverb

Deep friendship requires cultivation
over the years — evenings before the fire,
long walks together, and lots of time for talk.
Alan Loy McGinnis

ભ

There is no friend like the old friend
Who has shared our morning days,
No greeting like his welcome,
No homage like his praise;
Fame is the scentless sunflower
With gaudy crown of gold;
But friendship is the breathing rose,
With sweets in every fold.

OLIVER WENDELL HOLMES

Anyone who has ever attended
a college reunion knows how easily
two friends who haven't seen each other
for years can pick up the thread of
a conversation as if they had just flung
it down, like a skirt they had been hemming,
to answer the doorbell.

Phyllis Theroux

Friendship is precious,
not only in the shade, but in the sunshine of
life; and thanks to a benevolent arrangement
of things, the greater part of life is sunshine.

Thomas Jefferson

My first friend was my mother.
She taught me my first lessons about
friendship by being my first, last, and
most enduring friend, and even though
she is gone from this earth, she is far
from gone from my life.

Gloria Gaither

ᢒᣒ

What made us friends in the long ago
When we first met?
Well, I think I know;
The best in me and the best in you
Hailed each other because they knew
That always and always since life began
Our being friends was part of God's plan.

GEORGE WEBSTER DOUGLAS

Friendship is not diminished by distance
or time . . . by suffering or silence.
It is in these things that it roots most deeply.
It is from these things that it flowers.

Pam Brown

All that is worth cherishing
begins in the heart.

Suzanne Chapin

True friendships are lasting
because true love is eternal.
A friendship in which heart speaks
to heart is a gift from God.

Henri J. M. Nouwen

Once we have friends as part of our lives,
we are no longer the same.

James Osterhaus

❧

Trials that come into a person's life have a way of separating the genuine from the artificial. And so it is with friendship. In order to find out who are truly a man's friends, put him through a severe time of testing and stress, and his true friends will be there.

JAMES OSTERHAUS

Nothing can match the treasure
of common memories, of trials
endured together, of quarrels and
reconciliations and generous emotions.
Antoine de Saint-Exupery

Good company in a journey
makes the way seem shorter.
Izaak Walton

Kind words are jewels that live
in the heart and soul and remain
as blessed memories years after
they have been spoken.
Marvea Johnson

The place where two friends first met
is sacred to them all through their
friendship, all the more sacred as their
friendship deepens and grows old.
Phillips Brooks

ભ

My coat and I live comfortably together.
It has assumed all my wrinkles, does
not hurt me anywhere, has molded itself
on my deformities, and is complacent
to all my movements, and I only feel
its presence because it keeps me warm.
Old coats and old friends are
the same thing.

VICTOR HUGO

Too late we learn,
a man must hold his friend
Unjudged, accepted, trusted to the end.
John Boyle O'Reilly

It is one of the blessings of old friends
that you can afford to be stupid with them.
Ralph Waldo Emerson

Each year to ancient friendships adds a ring,
As to an oak.
James Russell Lowell

Time has a way of defining true friends.
I have discovered that passing years
and growing distance are ineffective
obstacles to the mutual love
between my friends and me.
Emilie Barnes

ॐ

There are three things that
grow more precious with age:
old wood to burn,
old books to read,
and old friends to enjoy.

EARLY AMERICAN PROVERB

As gold more splendid
from the fire appears,
Thus friendship brightens
by the length of years.

Ovid

Friendship — our friendship —
is like the beautiful shadows of evening,
spreading and growing till life
and its light pass away.

Michael Vitkovics

Depth of friendship does not
depend upon length of acquaintance.

Rabindranath Tagore

There is magic in the memory
of schoolboy friendships; it softens the
heart, and even affects the nervous system
of those who have no heart.

Benjamin Disraeli

ℭℜ

Where is the heart that does not keep
Within its inmost core
Some fond remembrance hidden deep
Of days that are no more?

ELLEN CLEMENTINE HOWARTH

It is easy to say how we love new friends,
and what we think of them, but words cannot
trace out all the fibers that knit us to the old.
George Eliot

And it is still true, no matter how old
you are, when you go out into the world,
it is best to hold hands and stick together.
Robert Fulgham

When we think of friends, and call their
faces out of the shadows, and their voices
out of the echoes that faint along the
corridors of memory, and do it without
knowing why save that we love to do it,
we content ourselves that friendship is a
Reality, and not a Fancy — that it is built
upon a rock, and not upon the sands that
dissolve away with the ebbing tides and
carry their monuments with them.
Douglas Fairbanks

CR

*Friendship is the shadow
of the evening, which increases
with the setting sun of life.*

JEAN DE LA FONTAINE

With every friend I love who has
been taken into the brown bosom of the
earth a part of me has been buried there;
but their contribution to my being of
happiness, strength and understanding
remains to sustain me in an altered world.

Helen Keller

No distance of place or lapse of time
can lessen the friendship of those who are
thoroughly persuaded of each other's worth.

Robert Southey

Friendship should be more
than biting time can sever.

T. S. Eliot

Friendships that have stood the
test of time and chance are surely best;
Brows may wrinkle, hair grow gray,
Friendship never knows decay.

Unknown

ଔ

*A day for toil,
an hour for sport,
But for a friend is life too short.*

RALPH WALDO EMERSON

NINE

Miscellaneous Thoughts on Friendship

In the fall of 1998, a "Hi and Lois" comic strip pictured a little girl named Trixie relaxing on a pillow in front of a window. She is thinking about a friend of hers: the sunbeam which shines through the window.

She muses that Sunbeam is cool, that it's not a he or a she, not black or white, rich or poor. In fact, she concludes, "Sunbeam's not even a person." But this brings a startling thought: "Come to think of it, I'm not sure I know *who* or *what* Sunbeam is!"

Trixie is soon comforted with this thought: "But I know a friend when I see one."

We have explored the meanings of friendship and been reminded that it is a rare and genuine treasure. We've pondered various definitions and descriptions, some of them profound, others very simple. And we've remembered the friends who have lasted through the years.

We just might need to settle back on the pillow with Trixie and admit that we really cannot adequately define friendship, but we sure know a friend when we see one!

ભ

I don't remember when I first began to call you "friend." One day the vague companionship that I'd seen grow so imperceptibly turned gold, and ran in tune with all I'd thought or dared to plan. Since then, you've been to me like music, low, yet clear; a fire that throws its warm, bright glow on me.

FLORENCE STEIGERWALT

Forgiveness swirls around all of our friendships. It is a powerful weeder and fertilizer, able to pull out the destructive elements that breed between friends, while deepening the roots that bind us together.

James Osterhaus

Friendships take time to season into trust. Like water in a deep well, honest expressions of the heart bubble up to the surface rather slowly. A man could go all his life and never taste the cold, bracing refreshment from such a well.
But once you've tasted it, the tepid, surface stuff will never satisfy.

Stu Weber

I am often gently nourished by a friend whose quiet company provides wisdom and comfort for my spirit.

Joy MacKenzie

ॐ

Wealth may crumble like some shaken tower, but friendship still remains. Disaster and defeat may overtake us and, like a shadow, hide our star, and our ambitions turn to ashes on our lips; but friendship, like some guardian angel, rekindles and fans into life the hope which had almost fled.

YEOMAN SHIELD

Friendship is like a prism through
which the many variations of beauty
are revealed in our lives.

Unknown

We are all travellers in the wilderness
of this world, and the best that we find
in our travels is an honest friend.

Robert Louis Stevenson

A mile walked with a friend
contains only a hundred steps.

Russian Proverb

଴

The deepest of friendships will often overrule logic. The things that would normally come between people don't apply because we're friends. The points of irritation are governed by the relationship. And the steep prices sometimes demanded are simply worth the friendship.

STU WEBER

We are sometimes made aware of
a kindness long passed, and realize that
there have been times when our friends'
thoughts of us were of so pure and lofty
a character that they passed over us like
the winds of heaven unnoticed; when
they treat us not as what we were,
but as what we aspire to be.

Henry David Thoreau

Friendship that flows from the heart cannot
be frozen by adversity, as the water that flows
from the spring cannot congeal in winter.

James Fenimore Cooper

Friendship between earthly friends
consists much in affection; but yet,
those strong exercises of affection, that
actually carry them through fire and water
for each other, are the highest
evidences of true friendship.

Jonathan Edwards

ℭℜ

*Friendships are born, enriched,
and deepened in moments of
need and vulnerability.
When resources are depleted.
When the fires of courage burn low.
When the slats have been kicked out of a
man's long-held dreams. Friendships that
sprout from that sort of soil are the kind
that endure through the years. Like a
deep-rooted oak, weathering a thousand
storms, growing stronger by the day.*

STU WEBER

Listening is a magnetic and strange thing,
a creative force. The friends who listen to us
are the ones we move toward, and we want
to sit in their radius. When we are listened to,
it creates us, makes us unfold and expand.

Karl Menninger

The mind is rarely so disturbed but that the
company of a friend will restore it to some
degree of tranquility and sedateness.

Adam Smith

The everyday kindness of the back roads
more than makes up for the acts of
greed in the headlines.

Charles Kuralt

In good times and bad, we need
friends who will pray for us, listen to us,
and lend a comforting hand and an
understanding ear when needed.

Beverly LaHaye

ﳀ

A good friend isn't surprised by your mistakes. She expects them. Somewhere, fairly early in the relationship, a good friend will find out the truth about you. She'll witness your weaknesses firsthand. And it's at this point that your friend, if she's really a good friend, will decide to stick by you anyway.

CARON LOVELESS

The greatest service one can perform
is to be a friend to someone.
Friendship is not only doing
something for someone, but it is
caring for someone, which is
what every person needs.

C. Neil Strait

There is nourishment from being
encouraged and helped up by others
when we are weak. We are nourished
from feedback from friends whom we
trust and who will be honest with us.

Rich G. Buhler

Good friends make the roughest trail easy.

Charles M. Russell

Happy is he to whom, in the more
mature season of life, there remains
one tried and constant friend.

Anna Letitia Barbauld

ℭℜ

They might not need me;
But they might.
I'll let my head be just in sight;
A smile as small as mine might be
Precisely their necessity.

EMILY DICKINSON

To hear complaints with patience,
even when complaints are vain,
is one of the duties of friendship.

Samuel Johnson

To have a friend is to have one
of the sweetest gifts that life can bring;
to be a friend is to have a solemn and
tender education of soul from day to day.

Amy Robertson Brown

A poor man may be said to be rich in the
midst of his poverty, so long as he enjoys the
interior sunshine of a devoted friend. The
wealthiest of men, on the contrary, is poor
and miserable, if he has no friend to whom he
can disclose the secrets of his heart.

James Gibbons

Have a heart that never hardens,
and a temper that never tires,
and a touch that never hurts.

Charles Dickens

∞

Oh, for the love of a friend
whose voice and touch will rainbow
sorrows, diamond tears, making of
them gems of rarest joy; one who forgives
all my shortages 'ere asked to do so;
one who dares to the uttermost of human
imagery; one whose ship will cast anchor,
and throw out the life line of hope
when storms are near; one who forgives
in me all that I can forgive in myself.

MAE LAWSON

ℭℜ

*Oh, for the love of a friend
who can be made the sacred trustee
of my heart; one who is more to me
than the closest relative; one whose very
name is so sacred that I want to whisper
it softly; one who lingers near my door
in time of distress, and stretches forth
his hand, which is not empty or cold,
and who says little, but feels largely.*

MAE LAWSON

ભ

It's friendship that plays the music, pours the coffee, and opens the windows on this bus ride through life. Sure, you could live without it but . . . why should you?

STU WEBER

The friend on whose fidelity you can
count, whose success in life flushes your
cheek with honest satisfaction, whose
triumphant career you have traced and read
with a heart throbbing almost as if it were
a thing alive, for whose honor you would
answer as for your own — that friend,
given to you by circumstances over which
you have no control, was God's own gift.

Frederic William Robertson

True friendship is no gourd, springing
in a night and withering in a day.

Charlotte Brontë

What a pity that so many people are living
with so few friends when the world is full
of lonesome strangers who would give
anything just to be somebody's friend.

Milo L. Arnold

℞

"A friend in need,"
my neighbor said to me —
"A friend indeed is what I mean to be;
In time of trouble I will come to you
And in the hour of need
you'll find me true."
I thought a bit, and took
him by the hand;
"My friend," said I,
"you do not understand
The inner meaning of
that simple rhyme —
A friend is what the heart
needs all the time."

HENRY VAN DYKE

Friendship — real, solid, life-enriching
friendship — always takes the high road.
True friendship travels the straight path.
Friendship never leaves you in a trap.
It always pulls you out of ditches, bandages
wounds, dusts you off, washes you off,
and sets you back on a healthy course.

Stu Weber

They are closest to us who
best understand what life means to us,
who feel for us as we feel for ourselves,
who are bound to us in triumph and disaster,
who break the spell of our loneliness.

Henry Alonzo Myers

Friendship is a kaleidoscopic
and complicated thing; it affords
many possible grounds for suspicion
and offense, but a truly wise man always
finds it possible to avoid them or smooth
them over or put up with them.

Marcus Tullius Cicero

☙

Give me work to do,
Give me health,
Give me joy in simple things,
Give me an eye for beauty,
A tongue for truth,
A heart that loves,
A mind that reasons,
A sympathy that understands.
Give me neither malice nor envy,
But a true kindness
And a noble common sense.
At the close of each day
Give me a book
And a friend with whom I can be silent.

S. M. FRAZIER

Can miles truly separate us from friends?
If we want to be with someone we love,
aren't we already there?

Richard Bach

Every deed and every relationship is
surrounded by an atmosphere of silence.
Friendship needs no words — it is solitude
delivered from the anguish of loneliness.

Dag Hammarskjöld

The ultimate measure of friends is
not where they stand in times of comfort
and convenience, but where they stand
in times of challenge and controversy.

Charles Stanley

Friends remind us we are part of
something greater than ourselves, a larger
world, and the right friends keep us on track.

Barbara Jenkins

CR

Friendships take time to season into trust. Like water in a deep well, honest expressions of the heart bubble up to the surface rather slowly. A man could go all his life and never taste the cold, bracing refreshment from such a well. But once you've tasted it, the tepid, surface stuff will never satisfy.

STU WEBER

Think where   man's glory
most begins and ends,
And say my glory was
I had such friends.

W. B. Yeats

The heartfelt counsel of a friend
is as sweet as perfume and incense.

Proverbs 27:9 (NLT)

A friend is:
a push when you've stopped
a word when you're lonely
a guide when you're searching
a smile when you're sad
a song when you're glad.

Author Unknown

A part of kindness consists in loving
people more than they deserve.

Joseph Joubert

ᘓ

*My friends have made the story
of my life. In a thousand ways
they have turned my limitations
into beautiful privileges, and enabled
me to walk serene and happy in the
shadow cast by my deprivation.*

HELEN KELLER

Little acts of kindness which we render
to each other in everyday life, are like
flowers by the wayside to the traveler:
they serve to gladden the heart and relieve
the tedium of life's journey.

Eunice Bathrick

You let me rant and rave and ramble.
Time after time, you sat with me and
wiped my tears and washed my cheeks
and whispered the words,
"I know. I know. I know."
And because of you, I held on.

Caron Loveless

The presence of friendship — or its
absence — will mark our days until we
make our exit from this planet.

Stu Weber

ℭℛ

When good friends walk beside us
On the trails that we must keep,
Our burdens seem less heavy,
And the hills are not so steep,
The weary miles pass swiftly,
Taken in a joyous stride,
And all the world seems brighter,
When friends walk by our side.

UNKNOWN

The holy passion of friendships is so sweet
and steady and loyal and enduring in nature
that it will last through a whole lifetime.

Mark Twain

The true way and the sure way to friendship
is through humility — being open to each
other, accepting each other just as we are.

Mother Teresa

If you love someone . . . you will
always believe in him, always expect the
best of him, and always stand your
ground in defending him.

1 Corinthians 13:7 (TLB)

Friends lift our spirits, keep us honest,
stick with us when times are tough, and
make mundane tasks enjoyable.
No wonder we want to make friends.

Em Griffin

Quotations by Source

About the Author

S. M. Henriques, known to his friends as "Rocky," lives and writes in Jackson, Mississippi. He is a graduate of Mississippi College and New Orleans Baptist Theological Seminary, with 20 years' experience as a pastor.

Rocky and his wife Mary Ann are the parents of two children, Jennifer and Jonathan.

He is the publisher of *The Timothy Report,* an electronic newsletter for pastors, church secretaries, church staff members, and Bible teachers.

For information about *The Timothy Report,* address your e-mail to SwanLC@aol.com

Other books by S. M. Henriques distributed by Walnut Grove Press

God Can Handle It . . . Marriage
God Can Handle It Day by Day
God Can Handle It for Kids
My Little Book of Prayer